And Then There Were None

Agatha Christie

TEACHER GUIDE

NOTE:

The trade book edition of the novel used to prepare this guide is found in the Novel Units catalog and on the Novel Units website. Using other editions may have varied page references.

Please note: We have assigned Interest Levels based on our knowledge of the themes and ideas of the books included in the Novel Units sets, however, please assess the appropriateness of this novel or trade book for the age level and maturity of your students prior to reading with them. You know your students best!

ISBN 978-1-58130-680-4

Printed in the United States of America.

To order, contact your local school supply store, or:

Toll-Free Fax: 877.716.7272
Phone: 888.650.4224
3901 Union Blvd., Suite 155
St. Louis, MO 63115

sales@novelunits.com

novelunits.com

Table of Contents

Skills and Strategies

Thinking
Identifying attributes, analysis, compare/contrast, brainstorming, paradox, identifying stereotypes

Listening/Speaking
Discussion, interview, oral report, tape recording, role-playing, oral reading, courtroom simulation

Literary Elements
Foreshadowing, characterization, setting, simile, metaphor, figures of speech, suspense, complex plot, comparison of British & American English, dialect, ellipses

Comprehension
Predicting, summarizing, cause/effect, inference, main idea, sequencing

Writing
Description, report, play, letter, time line, clue cards

Across the Curriculum
Art—collage, floor plan, 3-D model; Social Studies—Morse code, maps; Research—Internet, reference books, autobiography, biography; Science—drugs and medicine, fingerprinting, weather

Information About the Novel

Genre: Mystery

Main Characters: 8 guests—Dr. Armstrong, Miss Brent, Mr. Blore (a.k.a. Mr. Davis), Miss Claythorne, Captain Lombard, General MacArthur, Mr. Tony Marston, Justice Wargrave; and the butler and housekeeper, Mr. & Mrs. Rogers

Setting: August 1939 on Indian Island off Devon coast in England. The shape of the island resembles a man's head. A modern, luxurious house was built by an American millionaire crazy about yachting and later sold.

Themes: Mystery, secrecy, human weaknesses, guilt

Summary

Ten strangers gather together on isolated Indian Island for a holiday hosted by a mysterious Mr. Owen who is not present. During their first night some dark and wicked secrets about each are revealed. Terror and suspicion begin to mount and then one by one they die.

Special Notes to the Teacher

The mystery novel, *And Then There Were None*, was originally published in 1939 under the title *Ten Little Niggers*. The title *Ten Little Indians* was used in the American Broadway Play in 1944. In 1945, Hollywood adapted the book to film and titled it *And Then There Were None*. The last title is the one used most often in the United States.

Prejudice against certain racial and ethnic groups was much more tolerated in the first half of the 20th century than it is now. A teacher may want to discuss this with the students. Ms. Christie often uses stereotypes in her works. In *And Then There Were None* there are prejudicial descriptions of Mr. Morris being Jewish on pages 4, 5, 95. There are racial slurs on pages 25, 73, 79. A teacher may choose to use these references for discussions about prejudices, stereotypes, and political correctness.

A teacher should be aware that Ms. Christie uses the word "damn" and its variations throughout the novel (pages 4, 5, 7, 9, 26, 43, 45, 55, 57, 79, 86, 93, 95, 132, 137, 139, 150, 167, 168, 184, 189, 195). There are numerous references to alcoholic drinks (pages 9, 28, 34, 36, 46, 61).

About the Author

Agatha Christie is considered the most popular mystery writer of all time. She is considered the world's best-selling author next to Shakespeare. Over two billion copies of her books are in print in 104 languages. Often called the "Queen of Mystery" and the "Duchess of Death," she penned over 100 mystery novels and short stories, 21 plays, a two-volume autobiography, and six romantic novels over a 55-year period. Agatha Christie's characters, Hercule Poirot and Miss Marple, are famous in literature, film, and television.

Agatha Mary Clarissa Miller was born on September 15, 1890 in Torquay, England, to an American father and English mother. She had an older sister, Madge, and an older brother, Monty. Her parents were affluent, but Agatha was not sent to school. She was often left free to amuse herself, and she invented her own companions and their escapades. Agatha loved reading and taught herself how to read by the age of five. Her father decided to teach her how to write and introduced her to arithmetic. A local newspaper published one of her poems about trams when she was 11, and when she was 17, *Poetry Review* published a few of her poems.

Her father died when she was 11 leaving the family less well off than thought. Her widowed mother did manage to send Agatha to France to study music and piano. Agatha had ambitions to be a singer or concert pianist, but she discovered she lacked the determination and self-control to be a performer. She had her debut to society in Cairo rather than in London due to the costs.

When she returned to England after her French and Cairo education, her mother encouraged her to attend country house parties where she was exposed to upper-middle-class English social eccentricities. She met Archibald "Archie" Christie, from Clifton, a junior officer in the Flying Corps. They were soon engaged, but postponed their marriage for two years because of the war. While Archie was away training, Agatha became involved in first aid and home nursing classes. She was assigned to a hospital in Torquay as a voluntary nurse's aide. Archie and Agatha were married on December 24, 1914, when he was home on a three-day leave. He left immediately for a six-month service in Havel. She returned to live with her mother and resume her work in the hospital, first in the surgical ward and then in the dispensary.

Her sister challenged her to write a detective story in 1916 with her extra time. In two weeks she finished *The Mysterious Affair at Styles.* After editing, she sent the manuscript to four or five publishers, and it was rejected by all of them. She finally sent it to Mr. John Lane at Bodley Head, but did not hear from him. She discovered she was pregnant and gave birth to her daughter, Rosalind. Almost a year later, she heard from Mr. Lane that her novel would be published, and he offered her a contract for five more novels. A newspaper asked for the newspaper rights to publish her first book in installments for 50 pounds. This encouraged her to write more.

In 1925, her mother died and Archie told her he was interested in another woman. Heartbroken and depressed, she disappeared for ten days. With her marriage over and her mother gone, she dedicated herself to writing and changed from being an amateur writer to a professional writer. In 1928, after her daughter was in school, she resumed her love for travel. She visited the Near East on the Orient Express. In Baghdad and Damascus she visited archeological digs and became friends with the archeologists. It was during these travels that she met Mr. Max Mallowan. They were married in Edinburgh in 1930. He was 14 years younger than she, yet their marriage was a successful one and lasted over 45 years.

She traveled with Max to his digs in Syria and Iraq and began producing two to three novels a year. These settings served as the backdrop for many of her novels. She wrote mainly detective novels but started adapting her earlier works to the stage as she felt plays were easier to write. She also wrote straight novels under the name Mary Westmacott. Her energy remained high until she was 81 when she fell and broke her hip. Queen Elizabeth named her Dame of the British Empire in 1971. Her health failing, she died January 12, 1976, and is buried in St. Mary's churchyard in Cholsey, Berkshire.

Some of her most famous titles are: *Murder of Roger Ackroyd* (1926), *Murder at the Vicarage* (1930), *Murder on the Orient Express* (1934), *The ABC Murders* (1936), *Death on the Nile* (1937), *Appointment with Death* (1938), *And Then There Were None* (1939), *The Mousetrap* (1952), *The Witness for the Prosecution* (1953), and *Murder She Said* (1964). Her autobiography was published after her death.

The Characters

Ten Characters on the Island Listed in Alphabetical Order

Dr. Edward George Armstrong: physician with a former drinking problem

Miss Emily Caroline Brent: 65 years old, daughter of a colonel, not married, often highly judgmental

Mr. William Henry Blore: alias—Mr. Davis; former police officer with Scotland Yard; allegedly lived in the colony of South Africa but visited Indian Island as a child; has a moustache and close-set grey eyes

Miss Vera Elizabeth Claythorne: coming to be a secretary at Indian Island on her holiday, P.E. teacher (games mistress) at a school; involved in accidental drowning of child in her care

Captain Philip Lombard: distinguished-looking older gentleman, small moustache, former officer in East Africa

General John Gordon MacArthur: retired officer with grey hair and moustache and faded blue eyes

Mr. Anthony James "Tony" Marston: playboy, drives a sports car, drinks often, likes to flirt

Mrs. Ethel Rogers & Mr. Thomas Rogers: hired to be butler and housekeeper at Indian Island; formerly worked for Ms. Jennifer Brady who died

Justice Lawrence Wargrave: retired judge, known as the "hanging judge," has frog-like face with tortoise neck; oldest character

Other Characters

Mr. Isaac Morris: lawyer representing the "owner" of Indian Island; made arrangements, paid the bills

The Owens: assumed to be unknown owners of Indian Island; they both have bad handwriting; referred to as Mr. & Mrs. Ulick Norman Owen, Una Nancy Owen, Mrs./Miss Oliver

Mr. Fred Narracott: owner of boat that takes guests to the island; carries over provisions for the island

The Setting

Devon: a county in the southwest corner of England just east of Cornwall. It is a popular place for a traditional family holiday by the seaside and famous for cream teas (Devonshire cream). There are many coastal resorts. Famous ports/resorts are Plymouth (where the Pilgrims set out for America), Exeter (major trading post and famous for a Gothic cathedral), Torquay (birthplace of Agatha Christie). The Devon coast is fringed with rocky outcroppings, some inhabited, some are not. It is said that Burgh Island between Plymouth and Salcombe is the model for Indian Island, where Ms. Christie, as a child, most likely spent summer days on boat trips from Torquay.

Indian Island: a small island off the coast of Devon in southwestern England; said to resemble the head of a Native American Indian; originally bought by an American millionaire. Rumored to be owned now by Miss Gabrielle Turk, Hollywood film star; or by Mr. Merryweather for a honeymoon; or by the Admiralty for secret experiments; or by Mr. & Mrs. Owens.

Introductory Activities

Choose one or more of the following activities to establish appropriate background before reading the mystery.

1. Ask the students to recall a mystery they have read. Jot down the titles of several (e.g., Sherlock Holmes, Nancy Drew, Hardy Boys, *Goosebumps*). Ask the students what these mysteries have in common and begin a web of the attributes of mysteries. Tell the students the web will be used again at the end of the unit to add to/verify/change based on *And Then There Were None.*

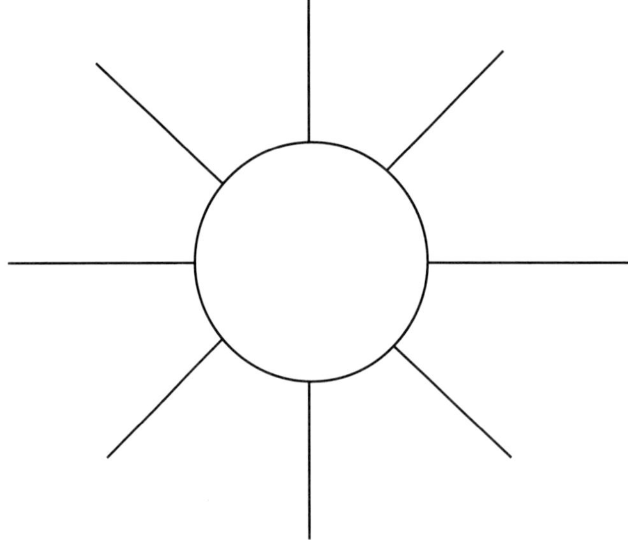

2. Read "About the Author" (see pages 3-5 of this guide). Discuss how famous Agatha Christie is and how her well-known characters, Miss Marple and Hercule Poirot, are famous also. Ask students if they have seen any of the movies/videos made of her novels. Discuss. Show photographs from *Agatha Christie: An Autobiography* (Putnam, 1977).

3. Distribute copies of the poem, "Ten Little Indians." Point out the last line of the poem, which gives the novel its title. Ask the students to predict what they think might happen in the book. (A copy of the poem appears on pp. 22-23 of the novel.)

4. Have the students set up a Prediction Chart to use as they read the book (see pages 9-10 in this guide). As the chapters are discussed they can update/change their predictions.

5. Have the student set up a Character Chart (see page 11 in this guide). The characters are introduced in Chapters 1-2, but more details can be added to the chart as more behaviors, traits, and background information are revealed in the succeeding chapters.

6. Make a class pact. Have the students promise not to reveal any of the happenings in the mystery if they should read ahead.

Note: The "Ten Little Indians" rhyme used in *And Then There Were None* is based on an American comic song and chorus by Philadelphia songwriter Septimus Winner, 1868.

Vocabulary Activities

1. Comparison Chart: Have students keep an ongoing list of words and phrases that they come across in the book that are distinctively British. Let them guess at the meaning based on the context of the sentence and describe how it might be said in American English or its equivalent in the United States. Some suggested terms/words/phrases for *And Then There Were None* are: driving his Morris (8), one over the eight (10), a southeasterly (19), *Punch* (30), these old salts (98), oh good egg (156). There are also differences in spellings in some words between the British version and the American version. Examples: colour (Br.) vs. color (Am.), offence (Br.) vs. offense (Am.), and armour (Br.) vs. armor (Am.).

2. Target Word Maps: Have students complete word maps for vocabulary words of a certain part of speech. For example, in *And Then There Were None*, adjectives would include: malevolent (16), rheumatic (54), impassive (89), bestial (143). Adverbs would include: covertly (48), obliquely (69), shrewdly (96), affably (122).

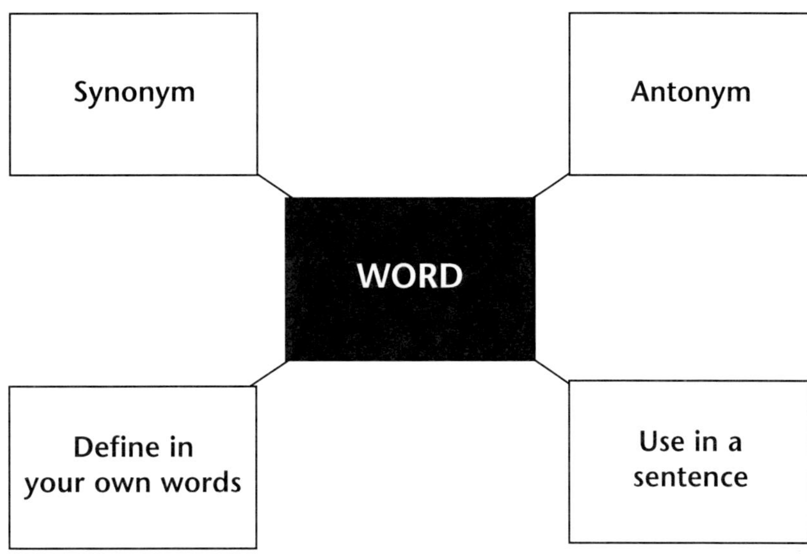

3. Vocabulary Sort: Have students sort vocabulary words into categories (e.g., nouns, verbs, adjectives, adverbs).

4. Sentences: Have the students select three or four vocabulary words and use as many as possible in one sentence.

5. Synonym Match: Have students select vocabulary words from a chapter and list one synonym for each vocabulary word on an index card. Students mix up the cards and match each synonym to the appropriate vocabulary word.

6. Identify Location: Have students study the locations mentioned in *And Then There Were None* and locate them on a map of Great Britain. Examples include Devon (3), Torquay (13), and Dorset (15). Ask the students why they think Agatha Christie would select these locations for the setting.

7. Figures of Speech: Have students start a list of the figures of speech in the book. Have them determine the meaning of the phrases through the context and/or information from a dictionary or reference book. Some suggested ones in *And Then There Were None* include "cat's out of the bag" (40), "bee in his bonnet" (44), and "wrong end of the stick" (44).

Using Predictions in the Novel Unit Approach

We all make predictions as we read—little guesses about what will happen next, how a conflict will be resolved, which details will be important to the plot, which details will help fill in our sense of a character. Students should be encouraged to predict, to make sensible guesses as they read the novel.

As students work on their predictions, these discussion questions can be used to guide them: What are some of the ways to predict? What is the process of a sophisticated reader's thinking and predicting? What clues does an author give to help us make predictions? Why are some predictions more likely to be accurate than others?

Create a chart for recording predictions. This could be either an individual or class activity. As each subsequent chapter is discussed, students can review and correct their previous predictions about plot and characters as necessary.

Use the facts and ideas the author gives.

Use your own prior knowledge.

Apply any new information (i.e., from class discussion) that may cause you to change your mind.

Predictions:

____

____

____

____

Prediction Chart for *And Then There Were None*

Date	Identity of Murderer	Reasoning

Character Chart for *And Then There Were None*

Character's Name	Occupation	Characteristics	History/ Background Information	Further Clues	Order of Death/Cause

Chapter 1, Pages 1-11

The first chapter introduces the reader to the rumors surrounding Indian Island and eight of the characters. The guests being invited to the island for the holidays are somewhat unsure of the identity of their hosts. Mr. Isaac Morris, a lawyer representing the hosts, is referred to negatively by Captain Lombard (see Notes to Teacher, page 3).

Vocabulary

recumbent (11)

Discussion Questions

1. After students have begun the Character Chart, ask them to compare and contrast the characters presented so far. There are references to the transportation modes taken by the characters. Ask: How could you use these references to draw conclusions about the characters? *(First-class train car [p. 2] and third-class train car [pp. 2, 5], non-smoking carriage [p. 5], slow train [p. 10], driving a Morris (an expensive car) [p. 8], and Dalmain (an super sports car) admiringly looked at by boys and men [p. 10].)* What other attributes mentioned about the characters help you know something about their backgrounds? *(Wargrave—retired justice, cigar smoker, reads political news [p. 1-2]. Claythorne—secretary and games mistress, coroner's inquest, Hugo, her lover [p. 2-4]. Lombard —interested in women, anti-Semitic, low on money, past actions may have been illegal [pp. 4-5]. Brent—65 years old, daughter of a colonel, critical of younger generation, righteous, reduced income [pp. 5-7]. MacArthur—impatient, something happened almost 30 years ago [p. 7]. Armstrong—a busy doctor, stereotypes women, former drinker [pp. 8-9]. Marston—drives fast sports car, drinker, a flirt [p. 9-10]. Blore [a.k.a. Davis]—allegedly grew up in colony of South Africa, visited Indian Island when he was a boy, a private detective [pp. 10-11].)*

2. Why do you think the characters are so willing to spend a week on an island when they are not sure of the hosts? *(There has been a lot of exciting gossip surrounding the island and its owner(s), which makes the invitation intriguing. The invitation comes in the summer when people traditionally take a holiday/vacation, pp. 1,2, 3, 7)* Why do you think there is such vagueness about the hosts? *(poor handwriting of the hosts left the guests confused; there are sketchy connections between the host and each guest that are not clear, pp. 2, 3, 5, 6, 7, 8, 9)*

Supplementary Activities

1. Have students begin the Character Chart and ask them to make note of the page number where a characteristic is mentioned.

2. Find England on a globe or pull-down map. Show students the map of Great Britain. Discuss the sections of Great Britain: England, Wales, Scotland, Ireland, Northern Ireland, outer islands. Ask: What kind of weather would they expect the area to have? Point out the Devon area in the southwest corner of England and tell students this is where the story will take place.

3. Ask students: What is a mystery? *(a story of suspense usually dealing with a puzzling crime)*

Chapter 2, Pages 12-27

The eight guests arriving by train or car travel from Sticklehaven to the island on a small boat owned by Mr. Fred Narracott. The guests settle into the modern house facing the sea with the help of Mr. and Mrs. Rogers, the servants hired for the holiday. In the bedroom of Miss Claythorne is a nursery rhyme, "Ten Little Indians," framed over the mantel (pp. 22-23). Each character is described more fully as they prepare for dinner and as Mr. Narracott sums them up.

Vocabulary

assent (12)	surreptitious (12)	assenting (16)	malevolence (16)
deuced (26)	cairngorm (27)		

Discussion Questions

1. Mr. Narracott, the boatman, sums up the characters on pages 18-19. Characteristics about each guest are also given on pages 23-27. As students add these characteristics to their Character Chart, do they find any connections between the characters? If so, describe. *(Dr. Armstrong knew Justice Wargrave, p. 24).* What characteristics of the setting given in this chapter foreshadow possible problems? *(wasps in summer, p. 14; hills, red earth, green and luscious, p. 15; fishing village with cottages near the beach, p. 16; rock on the island in the silhouette of a giant Indian's head with a sinister look, p. 16; house on south side of island facing south—low and square and modern-looking with rounded windows letting in light, p. 19; a southeasterly or summer storm can come up quickly and cut the island off from the mainland, p. 19; well-decorated house and rooms, pp. 20, 22; something magical about the island suggesting fantasy, p. 24)*

2. What is the significance of the children's rhyme framed in Miss Claythorne's room on pages 22-23? *(The "Ten Little Indians" rhyme was thought by Miss Claythorne to be appropriate as the island is called Indian Island. If students say it also foreshadows what will happen to the characters say, "We will see.")*

Supplementary Activities

1. Have the students add to the Character Chart.

2. Have the students begin labeling the map of Indian Island or draw their own version.

3. Have students pair up and read the rhyme "Ten Little Indians" aloud to each other (pp. 22-23).

Chapter 3, Pages 28-41

The guests are at dinner and have been told their hosts, Mr. and Mrs. Owens, have been delayed. The centerpiece at the table is a set of ten small china Indian figurines as in the nursery rhyme. The guests share that they each have the framed rhyme in their rooms. Suddenly a voice from an undisclosed place in the drawing room charges each guest with a crime. They are startled and alarmed and discover a gramophone and record are the source of the voice. Each guest discloses how and why he/she was invited to the island.

Vocabulary

angularities (30)	petrified (31)	habitual (32)	gramophone (33)
preposterous (35)	sedative (36)	impromptu (36)	verisimilitude (39)

Discussion Questions

1. The Judge says on page 41, "'...we have been invited here by a madman—probably a dangerous homicidal lunatic.'" Do you think so? Why or why not? *(Certain things are very suspicious. For example, the hosts are not present; the way the gramophone was set up and The Voice with the charges made against the guests, pp. 30-31, 34; the vague and mysterious way the guests were invited, pp. 37-40)*

2. Each of the guests received a letter of invitation from the owner of Indian Island and a mention of a mutual acquaintance was made. Why was this included in the invitation? *(Students may speculate that the mention of the mutual acquaintance might have made the guests feel like they must know the host, pp. 38-40.)*

Supplementary Activities

1. Have students add the additional clues given for each character to their Character Chart. Ask how people usually act when they have something to hide. *(secretive, quiet, serious, maybe flippant)*

2. Ask students to define "suspense." *(anxiety or apprehension resulting from mysterious, undecided, uncertain circumstances).* Ask: What elements of suspense has Agatha Christie used thus far in her mystery? *(secluded island, host unknown to the guests, host not on the island, the nursery rhyme and figurines, the gramophone, the invitations, the instructions to the servants, the background of each guest)*

3. What does the figure of speech, "cat's out of the bag" mean on p. 40? *(a secret is no longer a secret; everyone knows now what was to have been kept secret)*

Chapter 4, Pages 42-49

The guests continue to explain how they were invited to the island. They realize the host, Mr. Owens, knows a good deal about each of them. Each begins defending the charges made on the gramophone record against him or her. At the closing of the chapter, Mr. Marston takes a swallow of his drink, chokes, gasps for breath, and dies.

Vocabulary

incoherent (42)	enticed (42)	epistolary (42)	babel (43)
iniquitous (43)	tumult (43)	impulsively (44)	exonerated (44)
reconnaissance (44)	*pukka sahib* (45)	deferential (46)	covertly (48)
reproach (48)	dissentient (49)		

Discussion Questions

1. Why does Dr. Armstrong say to himself that Judge Wargrave is lying about knowing Edward Seton, who was charged with murdering an elderly woman? *(Dr. Armstrong remembers the publicized trial and a lawyer friend who said the judge "was dead against him." pp. 43-44)*

2. The following phrases do not literally mean what they say. They are figures of speech. What do they mean? "got a bee in his bonnet" *(a person who is hysterical, p. 44)* and "wrong end of the stick" (p. 44)

3. What are examples from the text of the emotions of the characters as they tell their stories and their reactions to the others' stories? *("Her [Miss Claythorne's] breath came fast...Marston growled...He [Wargrave] said, picking his words with care," p. 43; "In a clear cold voice the judge...Claythorne spoke in a trembling voice...she broke down, weeping bitterly...General MacArthur patted her shoulder...he barked out," p. 44; "His [MacArthur's] shaking hand pulled at his moustache...He said sternly...His amused eyes looked into her horrified ones...Mr. Justice Wargrave said acidly," p. 45; '...it wasn't my [Marston's] fault. Just an accident!'...Rogers, had been moistening his lips and twisting his hand...said...in a low deferential voice...'There isn't a word of truth in it, sir'...the man's twitching face, his dry lips, the fright in his eyes," p. 46; "Blore went purple...Blore said sulkily...Lombard laughed a sudden ringing laugh...Emily Brent glanced at him in sharp distaste and drew herself away a little," p. 47; "He thought...'I killed her, all right'...Her lips [Brent's] closed tightly... [she] said coldly, 'There is no question of defense. I have always acted in accordance with the dictates of my conscience. I have nothing with which to reproach myself'...There was an unsatisfied feeling in the air...She sat unyielding," p. 48)*

Supplementary Activities

1. Ask students to add the new revelations of each characters' past to the Character Chart. This information may help them later in solving the mystery.

2. Have students dramatize or read orally with expression the parts where the guests are reacting to and explaining the accusations (see Discussion Question #3).

3. Ask students to make a prediction at this point in the mystery of who killed Mr. Marston. Have them write the date on the Prediction Chart and write down their idea. Save for future reference.

Chapter 5, Pages 50-59

The chapter opens with the guests realizing that Mr. Marston died of asphyxiation, which was brought on by poisoning. The shaken guests retire to their rooms. More background information is revealed in the thoughts of Justice Wargrave, General MacArthur, and Miss Claythorne. Mr. Rogers, the butler, notices that one of the Indian figurines is gone from the centerpiece. Miss Claythorne recalls the nursery rhyme and that the first Indian died because he choked, the same as Mr. Marston.

Vocabulary

asphyxiation (50) brusquely (51) cyanides (51) inert (52)
rheumatic (54) discomfiture (57) rancour (59) veronal (59)
doggerel (59)

Discussion Questions

1. Do you think Mr. Marston was murdered or committed suicide? Why? *(both causes of his death are discussed but based on Mr. Marston being a "young Norse God in the prime of his health and strength" it is doubtful it is suicide, pp. 50-52)*

2. Foreshadowing is to present a suggestion of something that is going to happen. Find several examples of foreshadowing Agatha Christie leaves for the reader in this chapter. *(Mr. Rogers finds a china figure missing, p. 54; General MacArthur doesn't want to leave the island and thinks, "'Best of an island is once you get there —you can't go any further... you've come to the end of things'...He knew, suddenly, that he didn't want to leave the island," pp. 57-58; Miss Claythorne recalls the first two lines of the rhyme and sees the connection with Mr. Marston's death. She wonders if the rhyme foreshadows the next death, p. 59)*

3. The characters are in shock after watching Mr. Marston choke to death. What are the ways Agatha Christie describes their collective reaction in part II of this chapter? *("...the others were standing...shivering a little...everyone hesitated. It was as though they clung to each other's company for reassurance," p. 52; "...went upstairs, a slow unwilling procession ...[no atmosphere in the house] that was the most frightening thing of all...each of them automatically...locked their door," p. 53)*

4. Have students discuss what people do or how they behave when they rationalize and justify actions that may be questionable. *(make excuses, blame others, blame a situation)* Ask: How did General MacArthur and Miss Claythorne justify their roles in others' deaths? *(MacArthur—his wife was in love with Richmond, so MacArthur had a right to be jealous, p. 55; He sent Richmond to his death, "It had been easy enough. Mistakes were being made all the time...all was confusion and panic," p. 56; Claythorne —perhaps killing Cyril so Hugo, her lover, would gain wealth. "Cyril wasn't really strong. A puny child—no stamina. The kind of child, perhaps, who wouldn't live to grow up," p. 59)* Ask: Do you think they felt any guilt? Why or why not? *(Answers will vary.)*

Supplementary Activities

1. Ask the students to add information to their Character Chart regarding the pasts of Mr. Marston, Justice Wargrave, General MacArthur and Miss Claythorne. Add any clues about Mr. and Mrs. Rogers also.

2. Students may want to look up the definitions and uses of cyanide, prussic acid, and potassium cyanide (p. 51). Have them speculate how the poison got in Mr. Marston's drink when it was not in the bottles of whiskey or soda.

Chapter 6, Pages 60-70

The chapter opens with Dr. Armstrong dreaming when Mr. Rogers, the butler, wakes him to come and check Mrs. Rogers who will not wake up. They discover she is dead. The other guests are watching for Mr. Narracott to come with his boat from the mainland. Dr. Armstrong informs them after breakfast that Mrs. Rogers is dead. They speculate on how she died and who might have killed her. They realize that Mr. Narracott is not coming today. Another china figurine is gone, and now there are eight.

Vocabulary

cascara (62), desultory (63), squally (63), ruminating (63), tabooed (64), ejaculations (64), ironic (66), chastisement (66), solicitude (66), obliquely (69), balmy (69), frenzied (70)

Discussion Questions

1. Refer to lines 3 and 4 of the "Ten Little Indians" rhyme. *("One stayed up late and overslept and then there were eight")* How do you think Mrs. Rogers died? *(possibilities include heart attack, poisoning, shock, overdose, suicide, and other ideas that students may suggest)*

2. Explain the statement made by Justice Wargrave on page 66: "'...in my experience of ill-doing, Providence leaves the work of conviction and chastisement to the mortals—and the process is often fraught with difficulties.'" *(He means that people may explain an ill-done death as someone being struck down by an almighty power. However, it is usually ill will from another person. People are quick to place blame and make judgments about the deceased when the person is not able to defend himself/herself.)*

Supplementary Activities

1. Have students add to the Character Chart—include Mrs. Rogers' death, and more characteristics about Miss Brent, Mr. Rogers, and Dr. Armstrong.

2. Have students make a second prediction of who the murderer is on the Prediction Chart. Date it so they can refer back to it later.

3. Have students dramatize a section of Part II where the guests are worried (pp. 62-64). General MacArthur and the judge are pacing the terrace, Miss Claythorne, Captain Lombard, Mr. Blore are watching for the boat to come; Miss Brent joins them, and Mr. Rogers, looking ill, serves them breakfast. Have the students show the look of fear, the gestures of worry, the physical actions of anxiety as well as the tone in their conversation that portrays the same feelings.

4. Have students begin a time line of events. Use adding machine tape (cut in lengths 12"-18"). Start with "August 8, 1939, guests arrive on the island." Include gramophone accusations, Mr. Marston's death, Mrs. Rogers' death, and other important events. They will continue adding to the time line.

Chapter 7, Pages 71-79

The guests continue to discuss theories that might explain the two deaths and to discuss the other guests' stories related on the gramophone. There is speculation that someone else is on the island causing the deaths.

Vocabulary

acquiesced (71), chaotic (73), perplexedly (73), serenely (73), hypocrisy (73), condone (74), self-reproach (74), placidly (75), juncture (75), consultation (75), amyl nitrate (76), ampoule (76), stiletto (76), ferret out (79), forte (79)

Discussion Questions

1. Compare and contrast Emily Brent and Vera Claythorne, the two women still alive on the island. Use information from Chapters 1-6 as well as their conversation on pages 71-74. *(Similarities—both are single, both have been involved in someone else's death, both rode in third class so they are on limited budgets. Differences—Brent is much older; Claythorne has a job, Brent does not; Brent is much more opinionated and judgmental while Claythorne acquiesces [p. 72]. Brent talks with confidence while Claythorne is hesitant and confused [pp. 71-73]. Brent is "self-righteous...encased in her own armour of virtue," while Claythorne is "horror-struck" [p. 74].)*

2. What are the terms used to describe Mr. Owen, the mysterious, unknown, unseen host? *("One Unknown Lunatic at Large....Indian Island is to be isolated until Mr. Owen has finished his job....the man must be a raving maniac....He'll be dangerous...big bad wolf," p. 79)* Speculate on who you think Mr. Owen is. What are his motives? *(Accept reasonable answers supported with clues from the novel).*

Supplementary Activities

1. Ask two students to role-play the conversation between Miss Brent and Miss Claythorne on pages 71-74 and two more to role-play Dr. Armstrong and Philip Lombard's interchange on pages 75-79.

2. Have students make a third prediction on the Prediction Chart. Do you think there is one murderer? Date it. (Some students may consistently give the same prediction; some may change their predictions as they gather more clues.)

3. Have students add to the Character Chart any information they gathered about the characters in this chapter. (Example—the judge has an acute logical brain but is "inactive" as described on p. 79. Another example "Blore [is] a good man in a pinch," p. 79)

Chapter 8, Pages 80-92

The guests continue to theorize about the deaths and Dr. Armstrong, Mr. Blore, and Captain Lombard search the island for Mr. Owen or someone else. General MacArthur is acting mad and repeats that the end is near for all of them. They search the house and the cliffs for a place where the murderer might hide. The men find nothing, and conclude that the murderer must be one of the guests.

Vocabulary

indignant (81)	oblivion (82)	genially (82)	recess (84)
aversion (84)	impudently (84)	spasmodically (86)	incredulously (87)
primus (89)	impassive (89)	countenance (89)	furtive (90)
admonitory (90)	stealthily (90)	cavernous (92)	festooned (92)

Discussion Questions

1. Analyze General MacArthur's behavior in this chapter. What is he doing? *("The old man sat very upright, his eyes fixed on the horizon. He paid no attention...His oblivion of them made one at least faintly uncomfortable...[He] frowned...He said: 'There is little time—so little time. I really must insist that no one disturbs me...You don't understand...Please go away'...Blore [said] 'He's*

crazy,' p. 82; "...there was a queer mixture of questioning and apprehension in [MacArthur's] look...He stared intently at her for a minute or two...he said...'It's a good place...to wait...[for] the end...We're all waiting for the end...None of us are going to leave the island. That's the plan...[what a] relief,'" p. 85; "He shook his head vaguely. He looked puzzled and a little distressed," p. 86) He seems resigned that he is going to die on the island. Why? *(Perhaps he accepts the responsibility for sending Richmond, his wife's lover, to his death many years ago. Now he regrets his actions and realizes he has to suffer the consequences.)*

2. Where did the three men search for Mr. Unknown Owen and/or his accomplice? *(the northwest side of island where they found General MacArthur sitting, p. 81; the highest point of the island, p. 83; the cliff, pp. 84, 89; the house where they heard Mr. Rogers, thinking it was a stranger, p. 89; the manhole, pp. 91-92.)*

Supplementary Activities

1. Ask students to draw a map of Indian Island. Have them indicate the highest point where General MacArthur was sitting, the cliffs, the docks, the home with terrace, and the manhole. Have them make speculations about hiding places. (Some students may propose secret passageways. Accept these speculations at this point and other feasible ideas.)

2. Ask students to add to the Character Chart. (Examples—Captain Lombard has a revolver, p. 81; General MacArthur's behavior, pp. 82, 84-87; Mr. Rogers' actions, and other clues the students may interpret, pp. 89, 91.)

Chapter 9, Pages 93-111

The guests are anxious and on edge. There is bickering and accusations are made against each other. The tension increases. A storm approaches. General MacArthur is found dead after being hit on the back of the head. Justice Wargrave suggests that Mr. Owen, the host, is actually one of the guests. After examining the events of the last two days they all agree there is "a devil amongst us."

Vocabulary

trional (94)	perjury (94)	eventuality (96)	noncommittal (96)
shrewdly (96)	malicious (97)	discourse (98)	accord (98)
corroborate (102)	truncheon (103)	cosh (103)	compassed (103)
absurd (103)	hearsay (104)	remorseless (106)	draught (107)
idiosyncrasy (107)	recrimination (107)	heliographing (109)	whilst (111)
complicity (111)	reiterate (111)		

Discussion Questions

1. Discuss the meaning of the phrase "Forewarned is forearmed" on page 111. *(It means one is alerted to dangers and must take precautions and be on one's guard.)*

2. Each guest is questioned about his/her whereabouts and must defend his/her actions related to being alone at some time with one of the murdered guests. How would you describe their reactions? *("Blore said sharply," p. 102; "Lombard said irritably," p. 103; "Vera cried angrily," p. 103; "in a cold voice [Miss Brent] said," p. 103; "Armstrong sprang to his feet. He was*

trembling," p. 105; "Mr. Justice Wargrave...looking quite passionless and inhuman," p. 108; Most of the guests react emotionally while Wargrave and Brent are calm, even cold in their reactions.)

3. Read the third section of the nursery rhyme, "Ten Little Indians." How does this correspond to General MacArthur's death? (*"Eight little Indian boys traveling in Devon; one said he'd stay there and then there were seven." General MacArthur in Chapter 8 talked of not being able to leave the island off the coast of Devon, and said that he was waiting for "the end," p. 85.)*

4. Justice Wargrave says on page 105, "'there can be no exceptions allowed on the score of character, position, or probability.'" What does he mean? *(No one can be accused or excused because of his/her reputation, social class, or gender. The facts for each event must be considered.)*

Supplementary Activities

1. Detective Cards: Have students play and recapture the events that have taken place. Individually or as a class, write each event on a 3" X 5" index card. Example:

1. 8 guests and 2 servants	2. Rhyme in each bedroom	3. Gramophone accusations	4. Mrs. Rogers faints	5. Mr. Marston chokes to death—suicide, murder?

   Others might include: 6) Mrs. Rogers found dead in bed, 7) island search for Mr. Owen, 8) Lombard has revolver, 9) General MacArthur found dead, 10) Storm comes up, etc. Are there any patterns or connections between the events? Keep the cards to reuse as other events may be added to help solve the mystery.

2. Have students add new events to the time line.

3. After reviewing the events, ask students to make another prediction about who the murderer(s) is/are on their Prediction Chart. Date the prediction.

4. Justice Wargrave holds a courtroom-like examination of the events and asks for alibis from each guest (pp. 101-111). Legal vocabulary is used such as: corroborate (102), Counsel (102), specimen (103), exonerated (104), hearsay (104), misstatement (106), criminal offence (106), alibi (108), proof (108), evidence (110), summoned before the court (111), the summing up will take place now (111), complicity (111), court will now adjourn (111). Ask students to use these words in a scenario. (For example: Goldilocks is on trial for breaking and entering.)

Chapter 10, Pages 112-121

The guests are suspicious of each other and begin to silently make accusations and pass judgment on each other. The storm increases. Everyone retires for the evening and locks his/her bedroom door.

Vocabulary

hared (114)	fiend (115)	tenacious (116)	clichés (116)
listlessly (118)	skeins (118)	normality (118)	pall (119)
respective (119)	looking-glass (120)	extinguishing (121)	

Discussion Questions

1. In Part IV (p. 117) Miss Brent adds to her journal and sums up the latest events. She doses off before she completes her thoughts on who the murderer is. When she awakens she discovers that it is written, "The murderer's name is Beatrice Taylor." What is significant about this? *(Miss Taylor was a servant for Miss Brent when Miss Taylor discovered she was pregnant [pp. 73-74]; Miss Brent and Beatrice's parents condemned her and abandoned her. Beatrice took her own life in desperation by throwing herself into the river. Miss Brent's subconscious may have surfaced and she is feeling guilty for abandoning the poor girl.)*

2. How do the guests begin to pair up? Why? *(Lombard and Claythorne, pp. 112-115; Blore and Rogers, pp. 115-116; Armstrong and Wargrave, pp. 116-117. They each have a need to exonerate themselves and discuss the theories about the murderer with someone else.)*

Supplementary Activities

1. Examine Mr. Rogers' dialect on page 115 and the dropping of "h." "'One of us, 'is lordship said. Which one? That's what I want to know. Who's the fiend in 'uman form?...You've got an idea 'aven't you?'" Some students may want to try reciting the phrases. Have them compare the dialect differences to ones in the U.S. For example, dropping of the "r" in the New England area.

2. Read the fourth section of the rhyme "Ten Little Indians." Have students predict who the next victim will be and how the murder will happen.

Chapter 11, Pages 122-132

The guests awake late to find the butler, Mr. Rogers, and Miss Brent missing from the house. There are only six china figures on the breakfast table. They find Mr. Rogers in the wash-house dead with a wound from a large chopper on the back of his head. They wonder to themselves who could have killed him. More background information is revealed about Miss Claythorne and Mr. Blore.

Vocabulary

abated (122)	affably (122)	ascertained (123)	untenanted (123)
mackintosh (124)	uncomprehendingly (125)	laconically (127)	perseveringly (127)
penal servitude (129)	crimson (129)	*sang-froid* (130)	repressed (130)
gimlet (130)	unflinchingly (131)		

Discussion Questions

1. Why was Mr. Rogers chopping wood? *(to light the kitchen fire, pp. 124-125. Remind students this is 1939 and they are still using wood stoves to cook. There is an electric generator, but it is used for certain light fixtures in the evenings only.)*

2. What was Mr. Blore doing on page 125 with the flour sifter from the kitchen? *(sprinkling flour over the handle of the chopper, the murder weapon, to check for fingerprints)*

3. Why is Miss Claythorne "crying out in a high shrill, shaken with bursts of laughter" asking about bees and honey? *(She realizes the nursery rhyme is foretelling everything and that the fifth murder will be by bee sting. She becomes hysterical, pp. 125-126.)*

4. Look at the simile on page 131, "thoughts that ran round in a circle like squirrels in a cage." Think of other similes that could describe the characters' anxious state. *(as jittery as jello, wide-eyed like a trapped animal, nervous as a hummingbird, etc.)*

5. Which character is thinking which thought on pages 131-132? *(Answers will vary. Students should support their guesses with good rationale.)*

Supplementary Activities

1. Have students add to the Character Chart new information derived from this chapter.

2. Have students make another prediction about the murderer. Date it.

3. Have students add the wash-house to the map on the island, mark an "X" where Mr. Rogers was found dead and label it.

4. Have students analyze some of the literary devices in this chapter:
    a. metaphor—"lips drew back from his teeth in that curious wolf-like smile" (p. 122)
    b. simile—"that woman's as mad as a hatter!" (p. 127)
    c. metaphor—"your lack of imagination is going to make you absolutely a sitting target." (p. 129)
    d. metaphor—"can make rings around you anytime he or she wants to" (p. 129)

5. As a class, analyze the author's use of italics, dashes, and ellipses on pp. 130-132. What is the purpose? *(to give emphasis and to note hesitation or disjointed thoughts)*

Chapter 12, Pages 133-142

The guests agree to meet after dinner to discuss the details of what has happened and try to figure out what to do. Miss Brent says she is feeling giddy and sits quietly after dinner while the others clean the dishes. The guests find her dead from an injection in the neck by a syringe. There is a bumblebee buzzing outside the window. They began accusing each other of murdering her. They search the house and discover Captain Lombard's revolver is missing.

Vocabulary

authoritative (133)	giddy (133)	aback (134)	dank (135)
demeanour (136)	acquitted (136)	hypodermic syringe (137)	fraught (138)
sulphonal (138)	bromide (138)	bicarbonate (138)	corridor (139)
rucked (140)	cumbrous (141)	dint (141)	

Discussion Questions

1. Miss Brent hallucinates in her "giddy" state before she dies about Beatrice Taylor, her former servant. What does this mean? *(Miss Bent is haunted about not helping the girl in her time of need. Miss Taylor drowned herself, and Miss Brent feels she has come back from the river to make her feel guilty and take revenge, pp. 134-135.)*

2. The guests are feeling extremely suspicious of each other. What are indications of this in their actions? *(Miss Brent refuses medicine from Dr. Armstrong, p. 133; they all go into the dining room to get Miss Brent rather than sending one person, p. 136; the five guests go to Dr. Armstrong's room looking for his syringe, p. 138; Justice Wargrave proposes they put the revolver and medicines they have in their possession in a secure place, p. 139; they all go to Captain Lombard's room to find his revolver, p. 139; they conduct a strip search of each other and search the rooms for the gun, p. 140; they go to the pantry together, p. 141; they all go outside to find the syringe, p. 142; Justice Wargrave says, "'...let us be careful to keep together. Remember, if we separate, the murderer gets his chance,'" p. 142)*

Supplementary Activities

1. Ask students to make another prediction about who the murderer is and date it.

2. As a class, add information to time line and/or Detective Cards.

3. Read aloud the fifth section of the nursery rhyme about the sixth little Indian boy (p. 22). Look at the next two lines. Ask: How will the next person die? (Explain that Chancery is a former famous high court for England and Wales.) Write on the board the students' speculations about the next murder. Predict who will be the next victim.

4. Ask interested students to research the drugs and needle mentioned in this chapter. Describe what they are used for and what level of dosage is lethal. *(hypodermic syringe, cyanides, potassium cyanide, p. 137; trional and sulphonal tablets, bromide, bicarbonate of soda, aspirin, p. 138)*

Chapter 13, Pages 143-152

The guests are highly stressed and the instinct of survival is in the air. They are, in their thoughts, accusing each other. Miss Claythorne goes to her room and walks into seaweed hanging from the ceiling. She screams and faints. The other guests come to her rescue and realize Justice Wargrave did not follow them. They discover him in the drawing room in a scarlet robe and gray wig as if he is dressed for the courtroom. They find he has been shot in the head. Dr. Armstrong pronounces him dead.

Vocabulary

dinning (143)	pretence (143)	veneer (143)	bestial (143)
ferocity (143)	pursuer (143)	lithe (143)	pitiable (144)
gall (144)	tacit (144)	larder (145)	siphon (146)
aeons (148)	Chancery (152)		

Discussion Questions

1. Why do you think the murderer put the seaweed in Miss Claythorne's room? *(the smell of the sea and seaweed is to remind her of Cyril's drowning in order to frighten her and make her feel guilty, p. 147)*

2. Why is Miss Claythorne suspicious of the brandy? *(she refuses to drink, thinking it might contain poison as it did for Mr. Marston [pp. 50-51], pp. 148-150)*

3. Why would the murderer "dress up" the judge? Discuss the fact that it is the first of the murders that seems "theatrical." *(Answers will vary.)*

Supplementary Activities

1. Make a chart of the similes and characteristics on pp. 143-144 that compare each guest to a beast. *(Justice Wargrave—hunched and motionless like a wary, old tortoise; Mr. Blore—coarse, clumsy, slow padding animal like a boar; Captain Lombard—highly sensitive, light, quick, lithe, graceful with "lips curling back from his long white teeth" like a wolf; Miss Claythorne —injured bird; Mr. Armstrong—nervous animal)*

2. Compare the predictions students made in Chapter 12 (Supplementary Activity #3) about the sixth murder with what happens on pp. 151-152.

3. Agatha Christie uses ellipses (...) to show the silent, anxious thoughts of the guests after dinner (pp. 145-146). Which guest is having which thoughts? Have students look at their Character Charts. Working in small groups have them decide which character is thinking which thoughts. Discuss as a class. *(Answers will vary. Captain Lombard accuses Dr. Armstrong. Mr. Blore is worried about who has the revolver. Justice Wargrave is afraid of death and blames Miss Claythorne. Dr. Armstrong wants to wake up from the nightmare. Miss Claythorne is trying to stay calm, keep her head.)*

Chapter 14, Pages 153-165

The remaining weary guests try to guess why no one heard the shot that killed Justice Wargrave. They all go to their bedrooms to try to sleep. Captain Lombard discovers his revolver is back in his drawer. Miss Claythorne thinks back about her love for Hugo. Mr. Blore hears someone in the hallway and goes to investigate. Dr. Armstrong is missing from his room and there are only three Indian figurines on the table.

Vocabulary

farce (155)	barricaded (155)	brazen (156)	sagacity (157)
astuteness (157)	wont (158)	assailed (159)	chromium (160)
ebonite (160)	pluckily (162)	vamoosed (165)	

Discussion Questions

1. Mr. Blore, the ex-inspector, is described as a man with sagacity and astuteness (p. 157). What does this mean? How is his character important to the story? *(He is wise, possesses sound judgment, is crafty and shrewd; Answers will vary.)*

2. What is the weather like in this chapter? *(it has cleared and stopped raining, "There's moonlight outside. As clear as day it is," p. 164)* What implications does this have? *(Tomorrow, Mr. Narracott may be able to come in the boat with supplies and rescue the guests.)*

Supplementary Activities

1. Ask students to check their Prediction Charts. Does any student have a prediction of the murderer that is still viable? Discuss.

2. Look at the nursery rhyme's eighth section, "A red herring swallowed one and then there were three." What does it mean? Ask students to investigate the meaning of red herring as a figure of speech. They will need to look on the Internet or in a large reference dictionary in the library. *(A red herring is literally a type of fish that has been salted and smoked to a dark color. It was common to use this type of fish to drag across a trail to destroy the scent for training hunting dogs. Gradually, it became to mean any diversion intended to distract attention from the real issue.)* Have the students write out their definition.

Chapter 15, Pages 166-177

The remaining three guests discuss ways of calling for help and where and why Dr. Armstrong has disappeared. They begin to think the doctor is not dead but is trying to throw them off guard as a "red herring." Mr. Blore goes to the house for some lunch while Captain Lombard and Miss Claythorne stay outside heliographing for help. They hear a thud and cry only later to find Mr. Blore on the terrace with a crushed head. A white marble clock shaped like a bear is the murder weapon. They suspect Dr. Armstrong is still alive until they find him floating dead near the rocky shore.

Vocabulary

Morse (166)	quietus (167)	stolidly (168)	abortive (171)
obstinately (171)	bunkum (173)	visitants (174)	innocuous (174)
vehemently (174)	lassitude (174)	Priest's Hole (175)	cunning (176)
raucous (176)			

Discussion Questions

1. Discuss the analogy Agatha Christie uses with a zoo on pages 170, 172. *("'Don't you see? We're the Zoo...we [are] hardly human any more.'"; "'Feeding time at the Zoo! The animals are very regular in their habits.'" The guests in their state of worry, guilt, and nervousness are seeing the worst in each other. Refer back to Chapter 13 and the guests' "bestial types," pp. 143-144)*

2. Why doesn't Mr. Narracott return to the island? *(the weather is clear but the sea is still choppy and too risky for a small motorboat to cross, p. 166. Answers will vary.)*

Supplementary Activities

1. Miss Claythorne begins to think that something supernatural has caused the deaths (pp. 173-174). Ask students if they think that is possible. *(Let students discuss possibilities. Guide them to the conclusion that it is not caused by the supernatural as there are not any other clues related to this possibility. Agatha Christie always has her crimes derive from human frailties, revenge, or conceit.)*

2. The remaining guests realize that "Mr. Owen" or the murderer is one of them and think that Dr. Armstrong has tricked them. When Captain Lombard and Miss Claythorne find the drowned doctor they realize one of the other guests is still alive. Ask the students, Who do you think it is? Make one more prediction and date it.

3. Have students add events to time line and/or Detective Cards.

4. As a class project, use a small mirror and heliograph the SOS signal in Morse code.

Chapter 16, Pages 178-183

Captain Lombard and Miss Claythorne rescue Dr. Armstrong's body from the sea. They become suspicious of each other. Miss Claythorne grabs Captain Lombard's revolver and shoots him in the heart. Miss Claythorne is in shock and goes up to the house to rest. In her room she finds a rope hanging in a noose from a hook in the ceiling with a chair to stand upon. She proceeds to hang herself as the rhyme predicted.

Vocabulary

conjuring (179) menacing (179) fender (183)

Discussion Questions

1. Look at Prediction Charts. Ask students to discuss their last prediction. Have the students discuss the confusing ending since all of the guests are dead. Do they think Miss Claythorne killed everyone? Why or why not? *(Answers will vary.)*

2. Why did Miss Claythorne hang herself? *(her guilt became very strong over the drowning of Cyril so Hugo could inherit the money; her feeling that she was trapped; the last line of the rhyme predicted she would hang herself; people in shock often do strange things, p. 183)*

Supplementary Activities

1. Role-play the scene on the beach when Miss Claythorne and Captain Lombard are dragging in Dr. Armstrong and then they struggle with each other (pp. 178-181).

2. Research what happens to a person when he/she is in "shock" in medical terms. Discuss if these attributes fit Miss Claythorne's behaviors after she shoots Captain Lombard. *(Someone in shock is in a general temporary state of massive psychological reaction to bodily trauma; it is usually characterized by marked loss of blood pressure and the depression of vital processes.)*

3. Discuss the ending. What if Captain Lombard had shot Miss Claythorne instead? Would he have hanged himself? *(Answers will vary.)*

4. Have students add events to time line and/or Detective Cards.

5. As a class, predict what the police will think when they discover the ten bodies. *(Answers will vary.)*

Epilogue, Pages 184-193

The police from Scotland Yard investigate the deaths of the ten people on the island. Their investigation leads them to Mr. Isaac Morris who bought the island for a client, Mr. Owen, and helped order the provisions for the island, including the gramophone record. It is discovered Mr. Morris is dead from an overdose on August 8, the same day the guests arrived on the island. Further investigation reveals that Boy Scouts saw the SOS signals from the island and told people in Sticklehaven. A group of men went over the next day. Police investigate the scene and then investigate the deaths mentioned on the gramophone. Each of these deaths happened, and there are implications that the deaths could be premeditated or caused by carelessness. The investigators are still puzzled and offer several hypothesis but none are proven.

Vocabulary

wangle (185)	vindictive (187)	peritonitis (188)	scrupulous (188)
barbiturates (189)	opportune (189)	cryptic (190)	subsided (191)

Discussion Questions

1. Do any of the clues given in this chapter help you figure out how the murders were accomplished? *(Answers will vary.)*

2. Do you think the murderer also killed Mr. Morris? *("'Morris took an overdose of sleeping stuff...barbiturates...was [it] accident or suicide?...That death of Morris' is...too opportune!'" p. 189)*

3. Do you think, like the Assistant Commissioner, that someone else was on the island although the Sticklehaven people are certain no one else left the island before the rescue boat got there (p. 192)? *(Answers will vary.)*

Supplementary Activities

1. Ask interested students to research Scotland Yard.

2. Ask students to add the events of August 11-13 to the time line and/or Detective Cards. Review all the events from August 8th to August 13th. Can you find a pattern, or causes and effects to figure out the mystery?

Final Epilogue—A Manuscript, Pages 194-204

Justice Lawrence Wargrave wrote a manuscript explaining all the murders, put it in a bottle, and threw it out to sea. A fisherman, master of the *Emma Jane*, found it and sent it to Scotland Yard. In the manuscript, Justice Wargrave tells why he committed the murders, the three clues he left, and how he plans to commit his own suicide.

Vocabulary

sadistic (194)	abhorrent (194)	palpably (195)	exigencies (196)
incongruous (196)	G.P. (196)	inexorable (196)	résumé (197)
perforce (197)	assuage (197)	maudlin (197)	coping stone (198)
amoral (199)	Potassium Cyanide (199)	Chloral Hydrate (199)	incriminating (200)
intimated (200)	rendezvous (201)	soldered (202)	gainsaid (203)

Discussion Questions

1. Ask students: Were you surprised at the explanation? *(Answers will vary.)* Ask students to look back at their Prediction Charts. Did anyone suspect Justice Wargrave after he supposedly "died"? Discuss.

2. Justice Wargrave compares himself to an artist. Read the first 14 lines of page 203. His conceit leads him to divulge the details of his murder mystery. Discuss. What if Wargrave had not left a manuscript or no one ever found the bottle? *(Answers will vary, but most likely the case would have gone unsolved.)*

3. Wargrave says he conducted "an interesting psychological experiment" (p. 202). How did he know that guilt and tension along with the suggestions in the rhyme would cause the last three guests to react as they did? *(Answers will vary; He had been a judge for years and knew how guilty people react under pressure.)*

4. Discuss the paradox of Justice Wargrave's personality (pp. 194-195) with a T-chart like the one below.

Positive	Negative
strong sense of justice	sadistic delight in seeing/causing death
innocent person should not suffer or die	fascinated with crime and punishment
right should prevail	read detective stories and thrillers
went into law	daydreamed about ingenious ways to carry out a murder
became a judge	pleasure in seeing a criminal suffer

Supplementary Activities

1. Make a chart explaining how Justice Wargrave determined whom the guests/victims on the island would be.

   Example:

Guest	How Wargrave Knew About His/Her Past
Mr. & Mrs. Rogers	p. 196—a doctor told him he felt drugs had been withheld from Miss Brady by her servants
Dr. Armstrong	p. 197—

2. Discuss how and why Justice Wargrave administered his own death (pp. 203-204).

Post-reading Discussion Questions

1. How would your rate this mystery on a scale of 1 to 10 with 10 being the best? Why?
2. What did you learn about the English and their culture by reading this book?
3. Discuss why Justice Wargrave would mastermind the murders and then take his own life.
4. What have you learned about guilt and secrecy from this work?
5. Discuss the following from *Agatha Christie: An Autobiography* (1977): "I wrote the book after a tremendous amount of planning, and I was pleased with what I had made of it. It was clear, straightforward, baffling, and yet had a perfectly reasonable explanation; in fact it had to have an epilogue in order to explain it. It was well received and reviewed, but the person who was really pleased with it was myself, for I knew better than any critic how difficult it had been."

Post-reading Extension Activities

1. Read/act out the play, *And Then There Were None*. Compare the differences between a script and a novel. What changes did Agatha Christie make when she transitioned from author to playwright?
2. Investigate several Agatha Christie Web sites. Examples include:

   http://mysteries.com

   http://members.tripod.com/teamystery

   http://christie.mysterynet.com/

   Note: Please be aware that Web sites change. Use your favorite search engine to locate information on this topic.
3. Find out more about Agatha Christie by looking at the photographs in her autobiography and *The Life and Crimes of Agatha Christie* by C. Osborne (1990).
4. Agatha Christie did volunteer work during WWI in an infirmary and hospital pharmacy. She knew about drugs and medicines. Investigate the ones she uses in *And Then There Were None.* Create a chart with three columns: Drug, Type of Drug and Purpose, Misuse on Victim. Title the chart. A helpful source is *The Poisonous Pen of Agatha Christie* by M.C. Gerald (1993).
5. Read another Christie mystery and compare it to *And Then There Were None.*
6. Research series of books by Agatha Christie. Select from the Miss Marple books, the Hercule Poirot books, or the nursery rhyme mysteries.
7. Three versions of *And Then There Were None* have been made into films in 1945 (setting—Indian Island), 1965 (setting—Austrian Alps), and 1975 (setting—hotel in Iranian desert). The latter two received very poor reviews. Find the 1945 version to view and compare it to the novel.
8. Find out more about Agatha Christie's private life and her works. There is a seven-tape cassette series from Books on Tape titled *Agatha Christie: The Woman and Her Mysteries* by Gillian Gill, read by Donada Peters. Ask the public library for a copy.
9. Construct a story map of *And Then There Were None.* What is the conflict? When does the climax happen? Is there a resolution?
10. If you could interview Agatha Christie, what would you ask her? Make a list of questions.

Assessment for *And Then There Were None*

Assessment is an ongoing process. The following ten items can be completed during the novel study. Once finished, the student and teacher will check the work. Points may be added to indicate the level of understanding.

Name ______________________________ Date ______________

Student	Teacher	
_______	_______	1. Write a poem about a character and his/her "flaw."
_______	_______	2. Illustrate and display your time line.
_______	_______	3. With a partner, rewrite a scene from the novel as a scene from a play and perform it for your classmates. Use props and costumes.
_______	_______	4. Develop a character attribute web for Justice Wargrave or Vera Claythorne.
_______	_______	5. Write a detective or murder mystery of your own.
_______	_______	6. Draw a floor plan of the house on Indian Island. Indicate where different events took place and where things were hidden.
_______	_______	7. Make a recording of the record on the gramophone. Use appropriate background music.
_______	_______	8. Research and give an oral report on Agatha Christie with new information not already discussed.
_______	_______	9. Interview adults about Agatha Christie and her works. Present your findings to the class.
_______	_______	10. Make a 3-D model of Indian Island to put on display.

Overall Evaluation of My Work:

Teacher's Evaluation of My Work:

Notes

